Focus on Buyers

Focus on Buyers

Selling from Your Prospect's Point of View

Rebecca and Jeff Fritzson

iUniverse, Inc.
New York Lincoln Shanghai

Focus on Buyers
Selling from Your Prospect's Point of View

iUniverse, Inc.

For information address:
iUniverse
2021 Pine Lake Road, Suite 100
Lincoln, NE 68512
www.iuniverse.com

ISBN: 0-595-29462-6 (Pbk)
ISBN: 0-595-66005-3 (Cloth)

Printed in the United States of America

Contents

1. Introduction

Have you ever wondered why your prospects acted the way they did? Have you ever lost a sale that you were convinced was a sure thing? Most sales people, at one time or another, are confused by the actions of their customers. Buyers—as we'll refer to prospects or customers, regardless of their job title within their own organization—don't always do what we expect. That's because most of us focus on our own needs as sellers, rather than focus on the needs of our buyers.

The most important aspect of this is an understanding of the steps your buyers take when they make a buying decision. Learning to recognize where they are in the buying process and what they really want from you will help you focus on their needs. You will also begin to recognize when you are the number one choice for a specific buyer and when you are being used to help the prospect buy from someone else. If you understand the way your buyer communicates, you will be able to determine your buyer's behavioral tendencies and match your communication style to your buyer's communication preferences.

Experience-Based Process

The inspiration for this book comes from the thousands of sales people we have worked with over the years. We found that many sales people spend so much time worrying about where they are in the sales cycle that they forget to think about their buyer and where he or she is in the buying cycle. Once they understand their buyer's perspective, they become better sales people.

We have had the opportunity to teach these concepts all over the world. We have found the buying model to be consistent across all cultures, even in those areas where negotiation is a way of life. We have also personally implemented sales processes that use these concepts within multiple technology companies, Jeff as sales executive and Rebecca as sales trainer.

Whether we work with beginning sales people or senior sales executives, our students tell us they increase their personal sales and develop a better relationship with their customers when they *Focus on Buyers*.

History of selling

In order to understand the relationship between buyers and sellers, we must first look at how selling methods used today evolved. Many of our misconceptions of how buyers buy are based on the way buyers bought several decades ago. For example, how many of you think that if you show your product to a buyer, he or she will want to buy it? Many of us still believe this, because this method used to work so well.

Door to door selling

During World War II, people were denied anything new for a very long time. When the war ended, people were hungry for new products. Door to door sales people were very successful because most people bought their products as soon as they saw them. Who can forget the image of the vacuum cleaner sales person walking in the door, throwing dirt on the carpet, and vacuuming it up with the latest and greatest vacuum? This worked up until the 1960's when television began to play a major role in marketing. Suddenly, people saw a continuous stream of "new and improved" products. Television could reach a much larger audience than any door to door sales person. By the time the sales person reached a prospect, the prospect had already seen an alternate product and made a purchasing decision.

Mass marketing

Door to door selling gave way to mass marketing. The number of new product introductions increased dramatically. As a result, consumers were bombarded with so many new products that those products had little meaning. It was much easier to stay with something familiar than to choose from a large number of unknown products.

While companies were learning that the way to a consumer was through television, companies selling to businesses faced many of the same issues. The number of potential suppliers increased, and business buyers had to find a way to choose. At the same time, many of the products used by businesses were becoming very technical. Buyers simply didn't understand many of the products they were expected to buy. As a result of these two issues, the relationship between the buyer and the seller became very important.

Buyers began to rely on their sales person to help them make the right decision. Sellers promised huge benefits, especially with computer or software related purchases. Buyers believed they would reap these benefits, simply by purchasing the products. The sales person made it sound so easy!

Adversarial relationship

Unfortunately, many of the promised benefits of the 70's and 80's didn't come to pass. Sellers had underestimated the amount of work required to make the changes necessary to see the benefits. Most buyers blamed their failure on the sales person who sold them the new product. This created an adversarial relationship between many buyers and sellers.

Think about the people you work with. How would they describe sales people? Is the description favorable or unfavorable? Unfortunately, the most common adjectives used are pushy, sleazy, and slick. Most people know that these are not characteristics of all sales people, but that image remains. The number one stereotype in most people's minds is the "used car sales person." Logically, we know most sales people do not fit this image, but in many cases, we anticipate the stereotype. We are pleasantly surprised when someone is different.

Sales people live by Napoleanic Law: they are guilty until proven innocent. What are they guilty of? They are guilty of all the sins committed by previous sales people who have talked to their prospect. As a result, prospects meeting a sales person for the first time may assume that the seller is "just like everyone else—pushy, sleazy, and slick." This expectation makes the first contact critical for the sellers. The only way you can continue the relationship is if you can show the buyer that you are different.

How sellers sell

Goals of the Seller

When you see a new prospect for the first time, why are you there? Is your goal to find something your prospect will buy? In other words, are you there to sell something? Many sellers enter into a relationship with their buyer because they need to sell something, not because the buyer needs to buy. Sellers enter the relationship for their own personal reasons. Selling is their job, and they see that as their goal with every new prospect.

How do your buyers feel when they think you are there only to sell them something? Most buyers feel tense and uncomfortable. They go into the meeting telling themselves they don't want or need to buy anything. They are very skeptical of what the seller tells them. They make the seller "prove himself" before they even consider what the seller is offering.

Now think of situations where you are a buyer. Do you like to buy? Most people answer with an unqualified "yes!" People like to buy because it feels good. When they buy, they are taking action to solve a problem. So we end up with a situation where people like to buy, but they hate to be sold.

Conversation or presentation

The following scenarios describe two different salespeople and how they handle a meeting with a new prospect. Which one do you think is more effective?

Sales person A

Sales person A arrives at John Smith's office. She knows she has approximately 30 minutes with Smith. She spends the first 5 minutes introducing her company and describing a customer success that occurred last year. Then she spends the next 20 minutes asking questions about Smith's business. Smith talks most of the time and admits a business problem he is currently experiencing. *Sales person A* helps him see how he could solve his problem, if he had her product. Because of the time constraints, she doesn't have time to show him the product during the first meeting but arranges a second meeting to discuss it with Smith.

Sales person B

Sales person B is also meeting with John Smith. He also has 30 minutes scheduled. He spends the first 10 minutes showing the corporate slide presentation and the next 15 minutes going over every detail of the product. *Sales person B* was just getting ready to ask questions of

Smith when Smith cut the meeting short. He said he had another meeting to attend. He also asked *sales person B* to leave a catalog and brochure. *Sales person B* was thrilled to leave the brochure and catalog convinced that it was a successful call and that Smith wanted to buy something.

What is the biggest difference between *sales person A* and *sales person B*? *A* had a conversation with Smith; *B* spent the entire time presenting to him. The buyer never even had a chance to talk. Conversations get the buyer involved. They give the seller the opportunity to find out about the buyer's situation, before talking about the product. Presentations can be very boring for the buyer. Buyers look for "what's in it for them." If they don't find it, they respond with objections. In addition, if the buyer doesn't understand the seller's product, hearing about every feature of the product won't make the buyer want to buy. If the buyer doesn't have a need, the seller is wasting his or her time.

Focus on buyers

Sales person A focused on the needs of her buyer. She took the time to find out about the buyer's situation before she ever talked about her product. Her goal for the first meeting was not to sell something. Instead, her goal was to learn about her prospect and find out if he needed any of the products she sells. Once she found the need, she could demonstrate the product in a way that has meaning to her buyer.

When we focus on our buyers, we sell to them the way that is most comfortable for them, not for us. We put their needs before our own. Doing this allows us to overcome any negative images the buyer may have by proving that we're different. The most effective way to achieve this is to understand buyers and how they buy. Once you understand how they buy, you can orchestrate your sales cycle to provide buyers with the information most relevant to them at the time.

Self Test

1. Why is it important to understand buyers and how they buy?

2. Why do many buyers have a negative opinion of sales people?

2.

Overview of the buying process

How buyers buy

The best way for you to learn how buyers move through a buying cycle is to put yourself in the buyer's place. In other words, think like a buyer rather than as a seller. In order to make this easier, recall your thoughts and actions the last time you made a major purchase. We'll use an example of buying a house, but you can think of a car, a boat, a computer, or any other product that you consider a major purchase.

No need

Think back before you ever considered buying a house. At that point, you had no need for a new house. You either already owned one or you were not ready to make the financial commitment for such a major purchase. What would you say to a real estate agent that approached you at this point? More than likely, you wouldn't really listen to what he or she had to say. When buyers are in NO NEED, they have almost no interest in the product or the sales person.

WHAT CAUSES A NEED?

What causes a buyer to have a need? Remember your own experiences. What caused you to buy a house? Most people list something similar to the following reasons for making this purchase:

- My family grew and our house didn't.
- My income has increased and I need the tax deduction.
- I found a new job in a new city.
- We wanted to be in a neighborhood with better schools.

If you examine these reasons, you'll see that some type of change caused each one. Change is the catalyst that drives most purchases. Whether it is a change in personal circumstances, as it usually is when buying a house, or a change in the company or the marketplace, as it often is for commercial purchases, most need begins with change. Change creates a problem, and problems create need.

UNRECOGNIZED OR UNACKNOWLEDGED NEED

Once the change occurred, did you acknowledge it immediately? Did you recognize this need right away? Most buyers don't. They move from NO NEED to a state that we call UN-NEED. UN-NEED is when the buyer has an unrecognized or unacknowledged need.

Unrecognized needs occur when a buyer hasn't yet realized he has a need. For example, if you were renting an apartment and your income was increasing steadily, at some point it would make sense for you to consider buying a house. However, chances are that you would not realize this immediately. You would have an unrecognized need. This need may stay unrecognized for weeks, months, or even years before you decided to act upon it. The length of time you remain in this state will vary, depending on the urgency of the need. If you decided to buy a house because you were starting a new job in a different city, you might have an unrecognized need for just a few hours or days. The need is more urgent, so the time in this state is significantly shorter.

The other type of UN-NEED is an unacknowledged need. This occurs when the buyer realizes the need exists but has been unable to solve it. For example, if you wanted to be in a neighborhood with better schools, but all the homes are far too expensive, you would be unable to satisfy this need. You recognize the need, but you can't do anything about it. Rather than worrying about something you can't really solve, you decide to forget about it. It becomes an unacknowledged need. It will stay that way until something changes—you either find a new area that has less expensive homes in a neighborhood with good schools, or your income increases enough for you to afford the houses that are currently available.

NEED EVALUATION

Once the need exists, at some point the buyer will recognize it. Think back to that point when you decided it was time to buy a house. What did you start thinking about? Did you immediately begin to look at houses? Most people don't, until they've taken the time to evaluate their need.

There are two concerns for the buyer during this state. What is my budget, and what does my need look like? More than likely, before you started looking at houses, you started listing what features you needed in a house. Your list might look something like this:

- How many bedrooms?
- How many bathrooms?
- How big should the house be?
- How much land do we want?
- Where do we want to live?
- Do we want a single story or multi-story house?
- What special features do we want in a house?
- How much can we afford?

If you were like most people, the list of features was so long that your budget would have to increase significantly in order to afford everything on the list. You probably started trading out "nice-to have" features for the "must-have" features, in order to get a more realistic picture of what you were looking for. Only when need evaluation was complete were you ready to start seriously looking for a house.

SOLUTION SEARCH

Once you had a list of what you were looking for, along with an estimated budget, what did you do next? Did you call a real estate agent? Did you begin looking at the classified advertising in the newspaper? The next state the buyer enters is the SOLUTION SEARCH. In this state, the buyer is looking for a product that matches his ideal solution determined in the NEED EVALUATION state.

Think about when you bought your house. Before you found the house that you wanted, you probably looked at many houses. Did your list of requirements stay exactly the same? Most people begin modifying their list as they look at product after product (or house after house.) Did your budget change? Buyers are often willing to increase their budget in order to get more "must-have" and "nice-to-have" features. In fact, by the time buyers make their final decision, they usually purchase a house with about 90% of their initial requirements for about 115% of their initial budget.

As buyers get closer to making their final decision, their budget and requirements become less flexible. Buyers are less willing to make compromises as they near the end of this state. Once you find yourself inside a house that you know is perfect for you, you want it. In fact, any house you look at from that point forward is compared to it. And nothing changes your mind. You've made your decision. You've moved to the next state.

PERCEIVED RISK

Once you knew what house you wanted to buy, what did you start thinking? At this point, most buyers begin thinking about what could go wrong. What is the risk involved in making this purchase? You may have worried about making the increased house payment every month. Or you might have worried that you might not qualify for the loan. Perhaps you were concerned that someone else would make an offer before you had a chance. If you were buying a previously owned house, did you get it inspected? Why? You probably wanted to verify that the house was structurally sound, that it met the building code for your area, that all the appliances were in working order, and that there was no termite damage. In other words, you were concerned about what could go wrong with the house itself. All of these inspection points are perceived risks. By having an inspector check out each item, you were eliminating the potential risks associated with the house.

How did you feel after you made the initial offer? Did you find yourself vacillating between hoping the owners would accept your offer and hoping they would decline it? If you had to wait overnight for their answer, did you get much sleep? These are natural responses to perceived risk. Every buyer experiences it with every purchase. The length of time and severity of the risk are related to the buyer's perceived importance of the purchase.

There are two possible outcomes to PERCEIVED RISK. As a buyer, you will either decide that the benefits outweigh the risk, and you will proceed with the purchase, or you will decide that the risk is too great, and you will abort the sale. If you cannot overcome the risk by switching to a different product, you may give up and move your need back to UN-NEED where it will remain until something changes. If you do proceed with the purchase, you will move all the way back to NO NEED until another change occurs.

How organizations buy

Since organizations are made up of people, understanding how organizations buy first requires that you understand how individuals buy. The five states of the buying process: NO NEED, UN-NEED, NEED EVALUATION, SOLUTION SEARCH, and PERCEIVED RISK, are the first pieces of the puzzle. But it's also important to understand how buyers make their decisions. Buyers in organizations will consider personal and professional reasons when they are contemplating a purchase. They will base their decision on both emotional and logical criteria, and they will usually work with multiple suppliers before they make their final decision. Rarely do organizations allow a single person to make a major purchasing decision. Most organizations will require multiple approvers on any major decision.

Personal and professional reasons

When people make buying decisions for their company, they make those decisions based on a combination of what is best for the company and what is best for the individual. Some people will put their personal needs above the needs of their company. Many purchasing decisions have been based on what new products would look good on a resume. As we examine each buying state in more detail, we'll look at why buyers buy based on their behavioral tendencies. Understanding these personal reasons can help you address all the needs of the buyer.

Emotional and logical criteria

If you ask someone why she bought a particular product, most of the time she will respond with a list of logical points that led to her decision. Even though the only criterion she mentions is logic, is logic the only thing that entered into the decision? Think of the last time that you bought a car. When people asked you why you chose the one you did, what did you say? Most people respond with things like "it gets great gas mileage" or "the repair record is really good." But is that the real reason? Didn't you choose the car because you really liked it, and then you used all of the logical benefits to back up your very emotional decision to buy? Some people will make an emotional decision based on the seller; others will get emotionally involved with the product. Either way, once the emotional decision is made, buyers will search for logical reasons to back up the emotional decision. Each individual will use his own combination of emotion and logic to make a purchasing decision.

Multiple suppliers

If a buyer in an organization decides she wants a particular product, she normally has to get approval from someone else in the organization. When she approaches the approver with her request, the most common question asked is "Who else have you looked at?" The person responsible for approving the purchase wants to make sure that the buyer has compared the requested product with other items available.

Organizations make every effort to have more than one supplier available for any purchase. This is done for several reasons. First, unless a second product is investigated, there is no way of knowing whether the product in question is reasonably priced. Second, buyers want to make sure that they are getting the best product for their application. By looking at other products on the market, they can verify that the one they have chosen is the best fit. Third, buyers know that sellers can make mistakes, and they want to have another supplier waiting in the wings if this happens. And finally, experienced buyers will use multiple suppliers during negotiation. They will get the lowest possible price from the supplier they don't want, and use that price and the threat of a lost order to get a better price from the supplier they do want.

Some private sector companies and most public sector organizations have a legal requirement for multiple bids. This is done to protect the organization when faced with a purchasing decision.

The vendor whose product most closely matches the buyer's requirements at any moment in time is known as the *preferred supplier*. The *preferred supplier* may change many times throughout the sales cycle, as the buyer's needs change. *Secondary suppliers* are the additional vendors a buyer evaluates whose products do not match the buyer's requirements. The buyer will use the *secondary suppliers* during negotiation in order to ensure the best price from the *preferred supplier*.

How can we tell if we are the *preferred supplier* in a specific sales situation? The buyer will give us different clues, depending on the state he or she is in. We'll look at these clues in detail as we examine each buying state individually in *Chapter 5*.

Multiple approvers

As products continue to increase in complexity, organizations are using multiple approvers for almost every major purchase. Many companies set up a "buying committee" responsible for all aspects of the evaluation and purchase decision. As a result, sellers must deal with numerous people, each with his or her own reasons for buying or not buying. Since buying committees are typically made up of people from different levels within an organization, one of the challenges sellers face is determining who has the authority or influence to make the buying decision. This does not always follow organizational structure. It is not uncommon for a mid-level manager to have such respect that they have the influence necessary to make the decision go their way. Since we can't rely on job titles, we have created some terms to describe the types of buyer roles you may encounter.

End User

An *end user* is a person who actually uses your product or service. An *end user* may be at any level in an organization. The job title of an *end user* will be dependent on the product. It is possible to have a single person be both an *end user* and a *decision-maker*.

Most *end users* do not have the influence or authority to make a purchasing decision on their own. However, they often have the ability to reject a particular product or supplier. Because of this, it is very important to include the *end users* in your sales cycle.

Shopper

A *shopper* is a person who is interested in your company or your products but has not admitted any business problem to you. A person will remain a *shopper* until he or she has admitted a business problem. Almost all leads start out as *shoppers*. Many *shoppers* are from the lower levels of an organization and are looking for information and education about your products, without any real need for your products. As sellers our goal is to eliminate those without a need and turn the rest of the *shoppers* into *prospects* as quickly as possible.

Prospect

A *prospect* is a person who has admitted a business problem to you. He or she may not have the authority or influence to actually make a purchasing decision but does have a need for your product or service. People will remain *prospects* until they have agreed to arrange a meeting with the next level up in the decision making process or until you have determined that they have the authority or influence to cause an unbudgeted purchase of your products or services.

Promoter

A *promoter* is a person who has admitted a business problem to you and has agreed to arrange a meeting with the next level up in the decision-making process. *Promoters* may not have the authority or influence to actually make a purchasing decision, but they do have a need for your product or service and have agreed to help you throughout the sales cycle.

Decision-maker

A *decision-maker* is a person who has either the authority or the influence to cause an unbudgeted purchase of your products or services. In addition, he or she must have admitted a business problem to you. A *decision-maker* should also be able to arrange a meeting with anyone in the company with whom you would like to speak.

Self Test

1. Pick a product you've bought recently and describe how you moved through the four states of the buying process. What were your thoughts during each state?
   - Un-need
   - Need evaluation
   - Solution search
   - Perceived risk

2. Why do organizational buyers work with multiple suppliers?

3. Define the following:
   - *Shopper*
   - *Prospect*
   - *Promoter*
   - *Decision-maker*

3.   Buyer Behavior

How the Technology Adoption Life Cycle affects buyers

The Technology Adoption Life Cycle is a model for understanding how people accept new forms of technology. Traditionally, the market is divided into five categories, shown below. Geoffrey Moore, in his book *Crossing the Chasm*, separates these five categories into two groups, the early market and the late market.

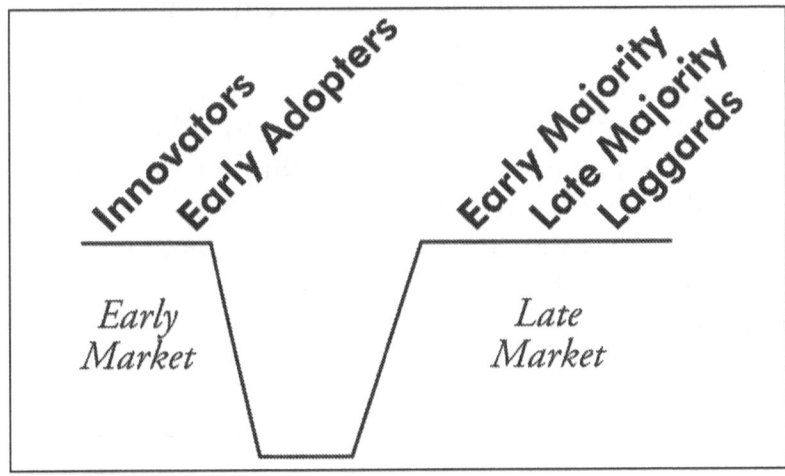

Early Market

The early market is made up of the first two categories: innovators and early adopters. People in the early market are the first ones to buy new technology. They are willing to put up with bug-fixes, software changes, and hardware upgrades in order to be the first ones with new technology. According to Geoffrey Moore, the early market is looking for some kind of change agent. Early market buyers look for ways to get a jump on their competition, and they are willing to try unproven technology to do this.

The people who make up the early market are the ones who understand the new technology and how it can be used. People who bought cellular telephones in the early eighties were willing to spend several thousand dollars in order to have telephone access in their car. Everyone else looked at cellular telephones as a frivolous product with little practical application. Why would anyone want to make a telephone call from the car? The innovators and early adopters saw a way to accomplish several things at one time. They knew they could spend driving time catching up on all their telephone messages.

The important thing to remember about the early market is that these people have the ability to figure out how they can use a new product. They will get excited about the technology because they will think of ways to use a product that designers never even considered. Innovators and early adopters will also respond to references, but they don't require them in order to make a purchase.

Late Market

The late market, composed of the early majority, late majority, and laggards, are looking for productivity improvements. They are looking for enhancements to their current way of doing business, rather than a completely new method of operation. While the early market will buy technology alone, the late market is looking for references showing how other companies have improved productivity.

The people who make up the late market do not care about new technology. They are much more interested in what they can do with it. Cellular phones are now selling mostly to the late market. Cellular phone companies have changed their entire marketing strategy as a result. Rather than selling a phone, they are now selling safety, family togetherness and productivity. Their advertisements focus on dangers that might require you to use a cellular phone, advantages of talking to family members on a moment's notice, and the ability to read email, send messages and receive phone calls on one device. One of our favorite commercials shows a woman in her car, stopped on the side of the road. It's late at night, and her car is not working. Another car pulls in beside her, and as a man slowly walks toward her, the voice-over says, "It's nice to think that if you ever have a problem, someone will stop and help. Unfortunately, you never know who it will be." This company is trying to sell cellular phones as a backup in case of emergency.

Millions of people now carry cellular telephones. Most of these people were the skeptics of the early eighties who couldn't think of a single reason why they would want to have a phone in their car. They are the late market buyers. They wait to see how others will use a product before they ever consider buying it.

Laggards, also considered part of the late market, are a special case. They are the people who may never buy technology. Do you know people who do not have an answering machine on their home telephone? They are the laggards. It doesn't matter how others have used a product; they have no interest in it. While the early and late majority will respond to application stories about a technology product, the laggards will often show no interest, no matter what the application.

The Chasm

Moore contends the result is that for every high-technology market, there is a chasm between the early market and late market. When a company tries to move from a customer base made up of innovators and early adopters to one made up of the early and late majority, it has a problem. The new market needs references in

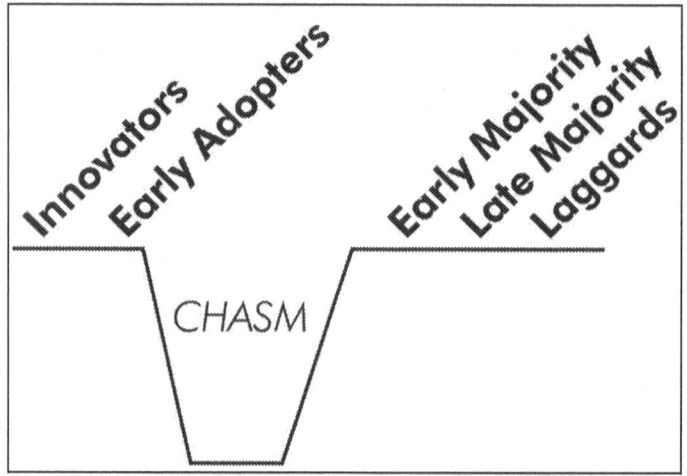

order to make a decision and it has very few references from the early market customers. The buyers in this new market purchase products and services that have already proven their benefits. This change in market also requires a completely new method of selling. Many companies have gone out of business because they didn't adapt quickly enough to their new market.

If you are selling to an innovator or early adopter, a product demonstration may be all that is needed, because these two groups create their own need and the solution for that need. Because they understand the technology and the products, merely seeing a new product will stimulate ideas on how the product can be used. Most high-tech companies start with this type of selling.

One of the reasons so many high-tech companies fail after a successful beginning is because they continue to sell by using product demos as they move into the late market. They still assume that their prospects will automatically understand how their product can be used. If buyers don't understand the products, as is the case with most of the late market, they will never see a need for the product. The sales person's job is to help buyers recognize a need and show them how the product or service is the solution to that need.

The other key to selling into the late market is the use of references. This market segment is interested in how other companies have been successful using a product or service. Stories about references are the perfect way to satisfy this need. The late market is made up of followers. They wait until other companies have tested and proven a new product or new idea. Stories about references are a way of communicating the accomplishments of existing customers to new prospects.

Late market and the buying states

People in the late market do not immediately recognize the purpose of a new product. They wait until others have purchased it and figured out how to use it. Once they see the success of others, they are willing to buy it. But it must solve a problem for them to even consider making the purchase. Here's how buyers in the late market progress through the buying states.

These late market buyers start out in NO NEED and move to UN-NEED when a change occurs. Once again, our buyer is in a state where she has a need but it is either unrecognized or unacknowledged. If our buyer sees a product, it means nothing to her because she does not understand how it would help her. If our buyer is told how someone else was able to solve a problem using the product, she will move from UN-NEED to NEED EVALUATION. In other words, our buyer is now ready to acknowledge that she has a problem. Once our buyer spends time determining exactly what she needs by determining the causes of the problem, she will move to SOLUTION SEARCH. Here our buyer is looking for the right product to satisfy her need. Once this is determined, our buyer moves to PERCEIVED RISK and then either makes a purchasing decision or moves the need back to UN-NEED.

Any buyer who is part of the late market or is an inexpert or novice buyer of the product will move through the buying states in this manner. This same situation will occur when the product is intangible or complex. If the product is intangible or complex, the buyer will not understand how it is used simply by looking at it. Whenever this situation occurs, the buyer will move from UN-NEED to NEED EVALUATION and then on to SOLUTION SEARCH and PERCEIVED RISK.

In order to see how this works, let's look at a simple product and see how buyers move through these states. For our example, we'll use a candy bar. Even though most of us are expert buyers of this product, we can still make purchasing decisions like a novice buyer.

Imagine that it's 3:00 p.m., you're sitting at your desk, and you're hungry. You've just moved from UN-NEED, before you recognized you were hungry, to NEED EVALUATION. During NEED EVALUATION, you will determine a list of requirements and a budget. Since you have limited access to food, you decide that your snack must be something from the candy machine down the hall. This, in turn, determines your budget. As you walk down the hall, you move from NEED EVALUATION to SOLUTION SEARCH. Your search begins as you evaluate all the choices in the machine. You narrow it down to two choices, potato chips or a candy bar. As you are about to make your final decision and choose the candy bar, you enter into PERCEIVED RISK. But what is the risk to a candy bar? Most people tell us the greatest risks in this situation are that you'll get fat or that the candy won't fall and you'll lose your money! These thoughts fly by in a split second and, before you know it, you've moved from PERCEIVED RISK to happy customer. At this point, you move back to NO NEED, until tomorrow when the snack attack happens all over again.

Early Market and the Buying States

We know that the people in the early market understand technology and can see how a product will be used. Let's look at how they progress through the buying states.

Everyone starts out in NO NEED. When a change occurs, our early market buyer moves from NO NEED to UN-NEED. Remember this is the state where the buyer has an unrecognized or unacknowledged need. In other words, our buyer has a need but he doesn't realize it. Our buyer sees a product, and immediately realizes what he could do with it. With this recognition, our buyer has moved from UN-NEED to SOLUTION SEARCH. As soon as he sees the functionality, he realizes he does indeed have a problem. Our buyer jumps from SOLUTION SEARCH back to NEED EVALUATION in order to justify the purchase. He realizes he has a problem, and he starts identifying all the details of the problem. Our buyer then moves back to SOLUTION SEARCH to compare other potential solutions, and then continues on to PERCEIVED RISK.

Any buyer who is part of the early market or is an expert buyer of a product will move through the buying states in this manner. This same situation occurs when the product is a very visual product. Anytime the buyer can look at a product and understand how it could be used, he will jump from UN-NEED to SOLUTION SEARCH and then back to NEED EVALUATION.

Let's use our candy bar example to illustrate how buyers move through the buying states in this order. This time, imagine that you just stopped off at the grocery store on your way home from work. You skipped lunch, and you haven't had dinner yet. You move through the aisles, picking out the groceries that you need, and have no plans to buy a candy bar. You are in UN-NEED. You're hungry, but you haven't acknowledged your need for a candy bar. You get in line at the checkout stand, and when you're next in line, you look over to your right. What do you see? Dozens of candy bars wait there to tempt you. You see your favorite, and you jump from UN-NEED to SOLUTION SEARCH. Of course, this is a very short search. You decide you want it, and to justify it, you jump back to NEED EVALUATION. You think, "I skipped lunch", or "I haven't had a candy bar in several weeks", or "It will be at least an hour before dinner is ready." You spend a few seconds evaluating your need, then verify that you selected the correct candy bar by spending time in SOLUTION SEARCH. This usually takes a fraction of a second, since you originally chose your favorite. The last buying state is PERCEIVED RISK where most people consider the fat content or the number of calories. There is that moment of indecision while you try to decide if you should buy it, followed quickly by your purchasing decision. You've just completed a buying cycle, and you go back to NO NEED.

Effect on buyer-seller relationship

Another way to look at the early market and late market is to look at the types of products that typically fall into these two categories. Many products will start out as an early market product. As they move through their life cycle, they eventually become late market products. Some products will even be thought of as a commodity—a product that can be bought from many different suppliers with little or no difference in functionality. Personal computers have gone through this market change. When first introduced, computers were considered a highly technical, specialized product that few people would ever own. The computer companies were selling to the early market. Today, personal computers can be purchased in most office supply or discount stores, and a very large percentage of families own a personal computer. Computers made the jump from the early market to the larger, late market. Many companies look at a basic computer as a commodity and select their suppliers based on price. As a result, computer manufacturers have come out with specialized computers, aimed at multimedia or networking. This is an attempt to attract the early market with the next generation of computers.

How does this affect the buyer-seller relationship? When a product is complex or intangible and the buyer doesn't fully understand it, the buyer will rely on the seller for the logical reasons to support the purchase. The seller acts as a consultant and guides the buyer through the buying cycle. The buyer relies less on the buyer-seller relationship and more on the information coming from the seller. Buyers buy from the sales person who understands their problem and their business, and how they could use a product to solve their problem.

When the buyer easily understands the product, the buyer doesn't need any help establishing the logical reasons to support the purchase. The buyer knows that he or she can buy the same product from several different suppliers. The relationship between the buyer and seller actually becomes part of the purchasing decision. In this case, the buyer looks to the seller for the emotional reasons to buy. The seller who offends the buyer loses the sale. How many times have you walked out of a store, even though you were ready to buy, because of something the sales person said or did? Have you ever bought something from a sales person, even though you weren't planning on buying anything? This happens because buyers become emotionally attached to sellers and will actually buy from the sales person they like the most. The seller's understanding of the buyer's needs is less important because buyers don't require the seller's expertise.

Self Test

1. Think of a product that you bought when you were an early market or expert buyer and answer the following questions:

   a. What was the product?

   b. How long had the product been available on the market, before you bought it?

   c. What made you realize you had a need for the product?

   d. What was the sales person's role in your buying decision?

   e. How many products did you compare before making your decision?

   f. What were some of the perceived risks you considered?

2. Think of a product that you bought where you were a late market or novice buyer and answer the following questions:

   a. What was the product?

   b. How long had the product been available on the market before you bought it?

   c. What made you realize you had a need for the product?

   d. What was the sales person's role in your buying decision?

e. How many products did you compare before making your decision?

f. What were some of the perceived risks you considered?

3. Is the relationship between the buyer and seller important in a commodity sale? Explain your answer.

4.   Determining Buyer Behavior Styles

How behavioral tendencies affect buyers

There are four main behavioral styles. In the DISC model, they are known as Dominating, Influencing, Steady State, and Conscientious. These styles are characterizations of someone's behavior, not their personality. Each person's behavioral style can change as the situation changes. Once you understand the four behaviors, you can use the information to improve your communication with your buyers as well as develop a greater understanding of why they buy. The first step in using this information is to determine the primary behavioral style of the person with whom you are working.

The Dominating Tendency

People who have a high D are one of the easiest styles to recognize. Everything happens at a faster pace for these individuals. They think fast and make decisions very quickly. D's are motivated to get immediate results. They place their emphasis on shaping their environment by overcoming opposition to accomplish these results.

Dominant people like control. They enjoy taking charge of situations. Have you ever been involved in a meeting that was going nowhere? The dominant person is the one who steps in, takes over, and gets results. Even when he has no official control over the situation, the dominant person will often take charge.

If you want to motivate a person with a high D, give her many new and varied activities. D's hate to do the same thing over and over. They enjoy challenges, especially in situations that will test their abilities. From time to time, D's need a shock to get them back on track. They prefer opportunities that allow them to advance or that showcase their personal accomplishment. They will often be adventurous, sometimes even daring as they take on these new challenges.

Dominant people will question the way things are currently done. They won't buy into the concept of "we've always done it this way." D's are very good at solving problems, so if they see something that needs to change, they will work to make it happen. They sometimes carry this to an extreme. D's need to learn to accept the importance of existing limits and the established way of doing things.

People with high dominance behavior need other people who spend more time researching a situation before making a decision. Because D's make decisions very quickly, they may not have all the information they need to make the best decision. They need someone who is cautious, someone who will calculate the risks and weigh the pros and cons before committing. If they are balanced by someone who deliberates before making a decision, they will be more effective.

D's also need people who recognize the needs of others since they tend to focus on their own needs first. They are very self sufficient, and often think that they don't need other people. One of their biggest challenges is to understand that they do need others. D's have a need to verbalize their reasons for the conclusions they've drawn. Working with others gives them this opportunity. They also need to feel some type of identification with a group.

People with a dominant style find it very difficult to relax. They have a tendency to be "workaholics," and have difficulty pacing themselves. One of their challenges is learning when and how to relax. Mastering this will allow them to increase their effectiveness.

Since control is so important for the dominant, their greatest fear is losing control or having someone take advantage of them. When they are under pressure, they may show a lack of concern for other people's views or feelings.

The Influencing Tendency

D's are task oriented and operate at a fast pace. The influencing behavioral style is also fast paced, but is more relationship-oriented. People with a high I put their emphasis on shaping their environment by influencing or persuading others.

High I's like people. Their biggest fear is social rejection. They are happy when people like them, and worry when they think someone doesn't like them. They thrive on peer recognition. Applause, certificates, and other forms of public recognition and appreciation mean a lot to an influencer.

Because I's are so people-oriented, they work hard to ensure they make a favorable impression on others. They can be very entertaining, and they have a talent for generating enthusiasm for projects and ideas. High I's are usually articulate, and they love the opportunity to verbalize their ideas. They can talk their way out of almost anything. They prefer an environment that allows them freedom of expression.

Influencers enjoy participating in a group, whether or not it is work-related. They tend to have lots of group activities outside of work. They love to be around people and want as much contact as possible. If you look at the center of attention in any group, you're likely to find a person with strong influence. One reason is that high I's are very charming. People are drawn to them.

If influencers could pick their ideal environment, they would pick one free of control and detail. They would also choose to have coaching and counseling readily available. They want to get to know everyone they come in contact with, especially if they expect to see them frequently. They prefer relationships that are equal, rather than one-sided. They don't want to control someone, they want to convince others to follow their plan.

Since influencers are so interested in people, they can be easily distracted from their work. They need someone who will help them concentrate on the task. People who look for facts rather than feelings and who develop a systematic approach can be of help to the high I individual. The influencer can be balanced by someone who takes a logical approach, as opposed to the I's emotional approach. High I's also need someone who respects sincerity and will speak directly. Since I's focus so much on people, they need someone who prefers dealing with things rather than with people. They work better with someone who demonstrates individual follow-through.

Under pressure I's become disorganized. In order to be more effective, I's need to learn better time management, especially if they have low D or S. They should focus more on priorities and deadlines. If they have a low score on D, they may need to be more firm with others. Because they build such strong relationships with others, I's are often influenced by this closeness. As a result, they often need more realistic appraisals of others and objectivity when making a decision. Influencers prefer a manager who allows them to participate in goal setting and task assignment, rather than one who makes decisions without consulting them.

The Steady-State Tendency

High I's are fast-paced people who focus on relationships. People with a high steady-state tendency also focus on relationships, but they operate at a slower pace. S's place their emphasis on cooperating with others to carry out a task. They have a strong desire to help other people, and they are extremely loyal. A steady person will take longer to get to know you than an influencer will, but once he feels close to you, he will stand by you through almost anything. When an S is under pressure, he tends to be overly willing to give.

Steady-state people perform in a consistent, predictable manner. They are very patient, and they work hard to develop a stable, harmonious work environment. Because they are focused on relationships without the need to be the center of attention, they make great listeners. They are very good at calming excited people. S's don't like conflict, so they will work to resolve problems as quickly as possible.

High S's tend to develop a set of specialized skills. They like to be given credit for any work they accomplish, and they usually have a strong identification with a group. S's tend to settle into predictable routines. They are motivated to keep everything just like it is. They don't like change unless there are strong reasons for the change. Their greatest fear is the loss of stability brought about by change. Don't rush an S into making a decision too quickly. If rushed, an S will decide to keep things the way they are.

Steady people keep their work and home life separate. They don't allow their work to infringe on their personal life. They prefer an environment where they receive sincere appreciation from others.

Since steady people make decisions slowly, they need others who react quickly to unexpected change. They also need people who are flexible in their work procedures and who work comfortably in an unpredictable environment. People who have the ability to become involved in more than one thing and who can help the S prioritize their work are also helpful.

In order for a steady person to be more effective, they need guidelines for accomplishing a task. They work better with work associates of similar competence and sincerity. S's need encouragement of their creativity, as well as validation of their self worth. When asked to make a change, they need time to get used to the idea of the change. Steady people also need to understand how their efforts contribute to the total effort of the team. This will help contribute to their feeling of self worth.

The Conscientious Tendency

High S's are slower-paced people who focus on relationships. People with a high conscientious tendency also operate at a slow pace, but they are task oriented, like high D's. C's place their emphasis on working conscientiously within their existing circumstances to ensure quality and accuracy.

C's are very detail oriented. They will focus on key directives and standards. They think analytically, and will weigh the pros and cons before making a decision. Conscientious people will check their work—and yours—for accuracy. They analyze performance critically and place a high value on quality and accuracy. C's use a systematic approach to situations or activities. Conscientious people are motivated by correctness and quality.

Conscientious people don't like direct conflict. They use a very subtle or indirect approach when faced with conflict. They are very diplomatic with others, and prefer to work in a reserved, businesslike atmosphere. They like clearly defined performance expectations, with control over those factors that affect their performance. The basic fear for C's is a criticism of their work. When she is under pressure, the conscientious person can become overly critical of herself and others.

C's love to have an opportunity to demonstrate their expertise. They like to be recognized for their specific skills and accomplishments. They also prefer an environment where they are given the opportunity to ask "why" questions.

Since conscientious people operate at a slow pace, they need other people who can make quick decisions. C's need to work with people who encourage teamwork. They need people who delegate important tasks, and will initiate and facilitate discussions. C's can become over-focused on details, so they need people who will use policies only as guidelines and be willing to compromise with the opposition. Since high C's don't like conflict, they work better when they have someone who is willing to state unpopular positions.

In order for a C to be effective, he needs an opportunity for careful planning. He prefers to have an exact job description with specified performance objectives. He wants to know exactly when his performance appraisal is scheduled. Because he focuses on details, he needs specific feedback on his performance. C's need to learn how to tolerate conflict. They also need to learn to respect people's personal worth as much as they respect their accomplishments.

Observation

In many situations, you may be able to determine someone's primary behavioral tendency through observation. This method will get easier as you become more familiar with the four primary behavioral styles and practice determining someone's primary style.

The first step in determining someone's behavior preference is to decide if the person is very talkative or more quiet and reserved. If you feel like you are forcing someone to talk, he or she is probably an S or a C. If the person is very talkative, he or she is more likely a D or an I.

To separate D's from I's, pay attention to the way they talk. If they speak fast and very freely with a dominant tone, they are probably a D. If they seem very friendly and easy to talk with and they give you a chance to talk, they are probably an I.

D's tend to:
- Talk faster.
- Be more direct.

- Sound busy.
- Try to get to the bottom line.

On the other hand, I's are usually:

- Pleasant.
- More informal.
- Willing to allow you the time you need.
- Interested in names of other users (if you are selling to them).
- Interested in how something will help them and their people.

To separate S's and C's, you will carry most of the conversation. In order to determine which profile fits best, listen carefully to the way they answer your questions. High S's are more concerned with stability, while high C's are concerned with detail and accuracy.

S's will often:

- Speak slowly.
- Talk about the way things have been done "for years."
- Be concerned about what will happen if something goes wrong (warranties, return policies, etc.)

While C's will normally:

- Want to know technical details, specifications, documentation, or facts about everything.
- Have a serious attitude.
- Want you to prove any claims you make or facts you state.
- Point out any errors you make.

How change affects buyers

In organizations today, the most common reason buyers develop a need is change. From corporate initiatives like total quality management and reengineering, to external factors like increased competition and technology improvements, change has become a way of life for most businesses.

Types of change

The types of changes that businesses face are many and varied. The changing work force has caused many new considerations for companies. There are more professional applicants available, yet companies are realizing they must teach basic skills like math and reading to many of their employees. The workforce is more diverse, which necessitates a better understanding of a large number of cultures. These changes affect everyone in an organization.

Changes in technology have had the most dramatic affect on organizations. Computer power is constantly escalating. Anything bought today will be obsolete in just a few months. The Internet has made information instantly accessible to almost everyone. These changes in technology have placed a burden on nearly every employee and every organization. Everyone is struggling to keep up with the latest technology.

Competition has changed as well. Organizations are now facing competition from global companies as well as specialized entrepreneurial companies. Organizations that succeed in the future will be flexible and respond quickly to new competition.

Other forces for change to which organizations must adjust include economic shocks, social trends and world politics. In order to adjust, organizations will develop needs for new products and services. Buyers within those organizations will leave the state of NO NEED and move to either UN-NEED or NEED EVALUATION. But how does this change really affect our buyer?

How change affects people

Understanding change and how people are affected by it is very important. Since change causes need, our prospects who are in UN-NEED or NEED EVALUATION are experiencing change when we first come into contact with them. Change creates the initial need, and our products become their way of satisfying this need.

There are many different models for change. Adams, Hayes and Hopson describe a coping cycle that people go through when faced with change. This coping cycle has 5 different stages. Here's how we move through these stages when we're undergoing change.

Stage 1: Denial
In this stage, we are so comfortable in our current position, we have no desire to change. Even though we know change will occur, we deny that it is necessary. We refuse to acknowledge the need for change.

Stage 2: Defense
During this stage, we are willing to acknowledge that change will occur. However, we still try to keep as much of our old system as possible. We try to keep things the same, even while acknowledging the reality of change. As we begin to recognize that change will occur, we move into a period of uncertainty.

Stage 3: Discarding
During this stage, we begin discarding our old ideas that get in the way of our new position. We move away from uncertainty and begin to accept our new position.

Stage 4: Adaptation
We now begin to adapt some of our old processes to our new position. We continue the process of changing, until we adapt to our new position. This leads to the last stage.

Stage 5: Internalization
At this point, our new situation, which threatened us in *denial*, has now become part of our comfort zone. We have internalized the change and any new requirements it entails. We stay this way until the next change comes our way and the cycle begins again.

What this means to our buyer

We can combine the change coping cycle with the five buyer states. In this model, buyers learn to adapt to a new method as they move through the buying states. This combined model is pictured below.

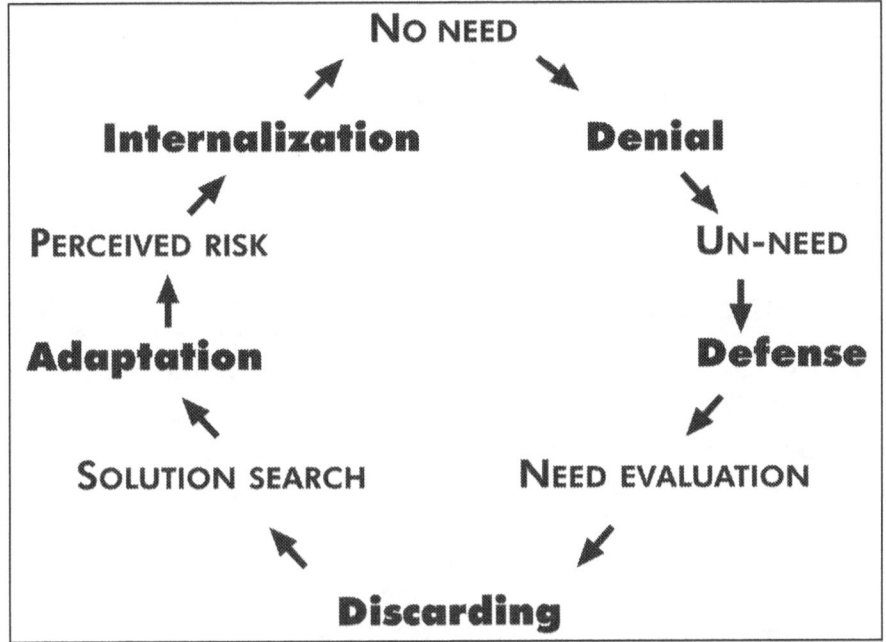

In order to understand this combined model, let's return to our example of buying a house. We start out in NO NEED, but as something changes in our lives, we move to *denial*. It might be that our family has grown and our house is too small. Even though we know this, we may still try to ignore it. As we are in *denial*, we move from NO NEED to UN-NEED. We have a need but we're not ready to acknowledge it. Stage 2 of the change coping cycle is *defense*. Here, we are willing to acknowledge our need to buy a house and we start our buying cycle as we move on to NEED EVALUATION. As we explore the type of house we need to buy, we solidify our list of requirements and our proposed budget, and we begin *discarding* any ideas, both old and new, that are in conflict with our change. We may realize that it is impossible to stay in the same area, or that the length of our commute will increase. At this time we begin to explore our options in SOLUTION SEARCH. We look at many different houses, until we find the perfect house. We move on to *adaptation* as we make our mental buying decision and change states to PERCEIVED RISK. Here we think about the negative and positive aspects of the house we want. We begin to mentally adapt to our change. As we make our final decision and learn to deal with our PERCEIVED RISK, we move into the final stage of the change coping cycle, *internalization*. Here we internalize our new position as we become comfortable in our new house, and we change buying states back to NO NEED.

How change affects the four behavioral styles

Each of the four behavioral styles views change in a completely different way. Understanding how buyers look at change will enable you to help your buyers move through the change coping cycle as they evaluate your products and services.

Dominant profile and change

People who have a high D are very results oriented. Because of this, they easily embrace anything new or untested. Think of high D's as *change-agents*.

Influencer profile and change

People who have a high I look at change as a way of life. They can be easily distracted, and because they become disorganized under pressure, they need someone to help them stay focused. Think of high I's as *change-creators*.

Steady State profile and change

People who have a high S have a strong need for security and stability. As a result, one of their biggest fears is sudden change. They will resist change will all of their might. Think of high S's as *change-resistors*.

Conscientious profile and change

People who have a high C value accuracy and order. They want to be certain about everything and are unwilling to experiment. They will try to stop any change until they can be positive everything will work, which is an almost impossible task. Think of high C's as *change-terminators*.

Self Test

1. A person with a high D makes his or her buying decision based on _____.

2. A person with a high I makes his or her buying decision based on _____.

3. A person with a high S makes his or her buying decision based on _____.

4. A person with a high C makes his or her buying decision based on _____.

5. A person with a high D is a change-_____.
   Why does this fit with their behavioral style?

6. A person with a high I is a change-_____.
   Why does this fit with their behavioral style?

7. A person with a high S is a change-_____.
   Why does this fit with their behavioral style?

8. A person with a high C is a change-_____.
   Why does this fit with their behavioral style?

5. Buying States

No Need

Buyers are in a state of NO NEED for a particular product when they already own a comparable product or when the product is of no benefit to them. For example, a person living in Florida with no plans for a winter vacation has no need for a pair of snow skis. Likewise, an avid skier living in Colorado will be in NO NEED if she already owns a pair of skis. If a new skier just bought a pair of skis, he will also be in NO NEED. All three of these people will remain in NO NEED until something changes.

What causes a buyer to leave NO NEED?

Buyers leave NO NEED because something about their situation has changed. We know from *Chapter 2* that change creates need. The change could be something that happens to a buyer that causes a need. If our skier has a skiing accident and breaks a ski, she will leave NO NEED. On the other hand, the change could be something that happens to the product. Upgrades to software create need in many people who are in NO NEED. Other product improvements may have this same result. Any improvement to an existing product has the potential to create need.

If the change is gradual, our buyer may move from NO NEED to UN-NEED. Gradual change is harder to recognize because we become comfortable with each intermediary step. For example, a company that grows by hiring one or two employees a month may not realize right away that the office space is too small. The owners may try to squeeze in a few more employees before they identify the need for a new location. They may stay in *denial* for a long time before they are willing to recognize that the change is necessary.

Instantaneous change is much easier to recognize because we move from a state of comfort to immediate discomfort. Buyers who experience instantaneous change are much more likely to move quickly from NO NEED, through UN-NEED, and on to NEED EVALUATION. Let's look at our example of a growing company. If the company suddenly has to hire 20 people, the owners are much more likely to realize immediately the need for more space. They may spend a few days in *denial* trying to ignore their need (UN-NEED). But if the change happens quickly and is significant, they will spend very little time in *denial* and UN-NEED and move into *defense* as they start NEED EVALUATION.

Un-Need

Buyers are in a state of UN-NEED for one of two reasons: they either have an unrecognized need or an unacknowledged need. Either way, when they are in UN-NEED, they are in *denial* about their need.

When a buyer has an unrecognized need, she hasn't realized that she has a problem. Many new products address unrecognized needs. Automatic teller machines have become a way of life for most of us, but twenty-five years ago, most people didn't think twice about the limited access they had to their banks. Even after ATM's were first introduced, many people couldn't imagine why they would ever need to use a machine when the bank was just around the corner. The early adopters for automatic teller machines were people who had an unrecognized need. As soon as they became aware of the service, they immediately recognized their need.

When a buyer has an unacknowledged need, he has tried to solve the problem in the past and was unable to do so. Since most people don't like to think continually about problems they can't solve, our buyer has rationalized his problem away. For him, the problem no longer exists. Let's look at a person in unacknowledged need. Our buyer currently wears glasses because he has a strong astigmatism. He has tried wearing several types of hard contact lenses but can only wear them for a few hours. Soft contact lenses are not made in his prescription and laser surgery is a risk he's not willing to take. To him, glasses are a problem, but he doesn't get up every morning and worry about it. He wears glasses because he needs to see. Since there are no other options available to him, he has rationalized away the problem and looks at wearing glasses as a solution to his vision problem. But what would happen if he hears about a new soft contact lens available for even the strongest astigmatism? He will immediately change states and enter NEED EVALUATION.

What is the buyer thinking about?

We know during UN-NEED that our buyer is not thinking about his problem or your products. He has other more pressing problems to think about. Psychologists tell us that most people can keep approximately 7 pieces of information (plus or minus 2) in short-term memory. This corresponds with the number of projects most people can manage at any one time. If more projects come their way, most people will drop something in order to manage the new project. Problems are like projects. If there is no immediate solution, the problem will be rationalized away and the person will change to UN-NEED. Our challenge as sellers is to get our buyer thinking about a problem that can be solved with our product or service. If we can accomplish this task, we can move our buyer from UN-NEED to NEED EVALUATION.

What causes a buyer to leave UN-NEED?

Remember our early market and late market buyers? These two groups respond differently when they are in UN-NEED. Since most of our marketing should be targeted toward people in UN-NEED, our target market will help determine the focus of our advertisement and direct mail campaigns. Advertisements that focus on the product with every feature explained in detail will have meaning to an early market buyer. That same advertisement will be completely ignored by a late market buyer. Advertisements that focus on problems and give the buyer hope will have meaning to both groups.

Late Market

Late market buyers will change states when they hear about the success of an earlier buyer. They will move from *denial* to *defense* in the change coping cycle. References, detailing how someone else used a product to solve a problem, are the most effective way of helping a buyer move to NEED EVALUATION.

Computers are another example of a product that has entered the late market. Thousands of people are buying computers today because they've heard of all the great things people in the early market are able to do. These same people are the ones who several years ago swore they would never buy a computer because they couldn't imagine how they would use one! The references from the early market that explained how people were using computers took these buyers from UN-NEED to NEED EVALUATION.

Early Market

Early market buyers will change states when one of two things occur: either they see a product and then immediately figure out what they could do with it or they hear a reference explaining how someone else was able to solve a problem using a particular product. As they move toward NEED EVALUATION, they, too, will go through *denial* in the change coping cycle.

By definition, early market buyers understand the product or service they are considering buying. They will get excited about the technology being sold. Product demonstrations can cause an early market buyer to change states into NEED EVALUATION. This is why so many companies use product demonstrations as their major interest generator. It works for the early market buyers, so they continue to use it, even when they are selling into the late market.

Early market buyers will also show interest when they hear how someone else has used a product. They will respond to references, just like the late market buyer. The early market buyer has the ability to understand both the product itself and the references from other users of the product. This makes our marketing job much easier. If we focus on problems and how our products help people solve them, both groups will respond. If we focus on our products, we're only reaching 20% of the total market.

How will the buyer behave toward sellers?

When a buyer is in UN-NEED, he doesn't think he has any reason to talk to a sales person. He doesn't have a problem (that he is aware of or has acknowledged) and he is not looking to buy anything. Since most buyers view unknown sales people with skepticism, they will be reluctant to meet unless they feel they have a need.

Behavioral tendencies and buyer behavior

Since our goal during UN-NEED is to move buyers into NEED EVALUATION, we will focus on what buyers are interested in when they hear about someone else who was able to solve a problem.

D's are very results-oriented, so they will be interested in the actual results the reference achieved. They have little interest in socializing, so you'll want to get to the point quickly with a D.

I's are more friendly and open, and they will be interested in who you have worked with. They will be interested in anything that can enhance their position within their company.

S's are afraid of change. They will want to know about your available support and how you helped the reference implement your products with as little disturbance as possible.

C's enjoy being the expert. They will question you on every aspect of your reference, wanting to know all the pertinent details.

NEED EVALUATION

Once the buyer changes states to NEED EVALUATION, she has actively started a buying cycle. Our buyer has acknowledged that she has a problem, and she is now trying to solve that problem. During this state, the buyer will determine a list of requirements and a budget. Some buyers will attempt to go through this state by themselves. Others will enlist the help of sales people to determine what they need.

Sellers should attempt to determine the symptoms the buyer is experiencing, what effects the situation is having on others in the organization, and what specific capabilities the buyer needs to solve his or her problem. These capabilities should be matched to the seller's product capabilities.

What is the buyer thinking about?

During NEED EVALUATION, the primary concern of the buyer is his need. He wants to determine if he really has a need, and if he does what his need looks like. The secondary concern for the buyer is the price of the solution. This is the reason why the

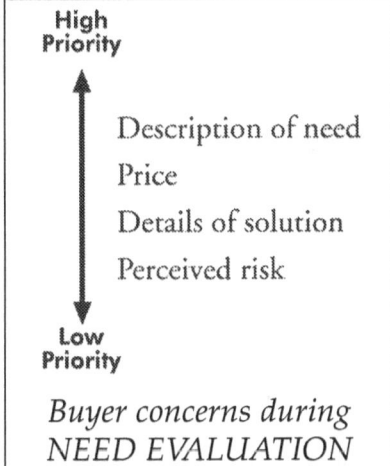

High
Priority

Description of need

Price

Details of solution

Perceived risk

Low
Priority

Buyer concerns during
NEED EVALUATION

question "How much is it?" follows so quickly after a buyer sees or hears about a product. As soon as the buyer knows what "it" is, he wants to know "it's" price. The third concern for the buyer is the actual solution. At this point, the buyer isn't thinking about the actual product; he is thinking about his personal requirements. The solution becomes a relatively low concern during this state. The final area is the perceived risk. During NEED EVALUATION, the buyer is not at all concerned with what could go wrong with his purchase—he's still trying to decide if he needs to make a purchase. Perceived risk is not a concern for our buyer during this state.

What causes a buyer to leave NEED EVALUATION?

Buyers leave NEED EVALUATION in one of two ways. When they have determined their list of requirements and their budget, they will move on to SOLUTION SEARCH. As they make this change of state, they will begin to discard their old way of doing things in order to prepare for the new way.

The second way buyers leave this state occurs when they determine that they don't really have a need. When this happens, buyers will move back to NO NEED. They will remain there until something else causes a buyer to change back to NEED EVALUATION.

How will the buyer behave toward sellers?

Earlier we discussed why buyers look at more than one supplier: they want to validate the price, they want to validate the product, they want an alternate supplier in case of problems with their *preferred supplier*, and they want an alternate supplier during price negotiation. Now we'll look at how buyers treat sellers when sellers try to diagnose the buyer's problem. The buyer's response is determined by the buyer's state—whether the seller is a *preferred supplier* or *secondary supplier*—and the action taken by the seller. We'll also look at how behavioral styles affect buyer behavior.

Preferred supplier versus everyone else

If the seller is the **preferred supplier** and the **seller tries to diagnose the buyer's problem**, the buyer will likely:

- Assume the seller fits the negative stereotype.
- Allow the seller to diagnose the buyer's need, after the seller has established competence.
- Answer the seller's questions openly and honestly.
- Have no deadline or specific time frame.
- Have no clear idea of how to evaluate the seller's products or services.
- Be willing to introduce the seller to the decision maker.

If the seller is **not the *preferred supplier*** and the **buyer has moved on to** SOLUTION SEARCH, when the **seller tries to diagnose the buyer's problem**, the buyer will likely:

- Try to limit the seller's access to information.
- Try to get the seller to make a quick diagnosis or accept the buyer's requirements with no diagnosis.
- Pressure the seller for a proposal.
- Limit the seller's contact with other members of the organization, especially the decision maker.

Behavioral tendencies and buyer behavior

During NEED EVALUATION, as sellers we try to set the buyer's requirements to match our product capabilities. To do this, we spend our time interviewing the buyer. Here's what we can expect from the four behavioral styles during this state.

D's will be less concerned with emotion and more with results. They will be very interested in what is possible and what the product capabilities can do for them. They won't really care how it works, only that it does work.

I's are more friendly and open, and they will be interested in who you have worked with. They will be interested in products that will enhance their position within their company. Any products that make I's look good personally will be favorable to them.

S's are afraid of change. They will want to know about your available support, and how you helped other customers implement your products with as little disturbance as possible.

C's enjoy being the expert. They will questions you on every aspect of your reference, wanting to know all the pertinent details.

SOLUTION SEARCH

During SOLUTION SEARCH, the buyer is trying to match her list of requirements and her budget to a specific product. As she moves through this state, she is finalizing her list of requirements. It is at this point that our buyer will call other suppliers to validate her purchasing decision. As she looks at different product offerings, she will add and delete items from her list of requirements. This will continue until late in SOLUTION SEARCH, when the requirements are set and our buyer is about to make her final decision.

If the seller has helped determine the needed capabilities based on his or her product, this state will be much easier to manage. If another seller has set the requirements to match his or her product, the buyer's SOLUTION SEARCH will be very difficult for the seller. The only way the *secondary supplier* can win is to become the *preferred supplier*. To do this, the *secondary supplier* must do one of two things. His first option is to match his product capabilities with the *preferred supplier's* product capabilities. He can then extend the solution with new capabilities that are absent or inferior in the *preferred supplier's* product. His second option is to change the solution completely. It is important to note that during SOLUTION SEARCH, the *preferred supplier* may change many times. A *secondary supplier* who does a good job of extending the solution with new capabilities will become the *preferred supplier* and the old *preferred supplier* will become a *secondary supplier*. What is important is who the *preferred supplier* is as the buyer nears the end of SOLUTION SEARCH.

What is the buyer thinking about?

During SOLUTION SEARCH, the buyer's primary concern is the solution itself. Buyers spend a great deal of time making sure that the product or service they are considering matches their need and solves their problem. Their secondary concern is the description of their need. Since buyers make changes to their requirements during this state, it follows that they will reevaluate their needs to make sure that the changes are in line with their goals. PERCEIVED RISK is initially low, but as the buyer gets closer to a final decision, PERCEIVED RISK becomes a higher priority. Concern over the price of the solution is at its lowest point during SOLUTION SEARCH. That's the reason that many buyers eventually pay more for an item than they originally had planned. As they make changes to their initial requirements, the price of the product increases. Because solution is of greater concern than price, most buyers will pay more.

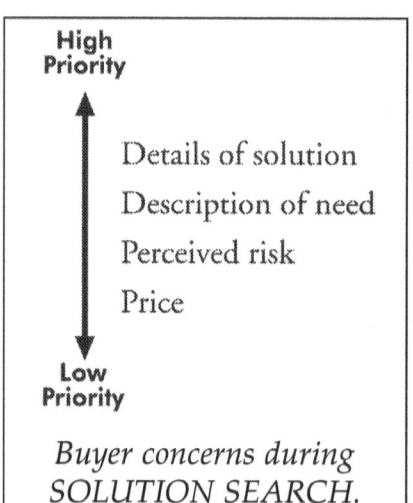

High
Priority

Details of solution

Description of need

Perceived risk

Price

Low
Priority

Buyer concerns during SOLUTION SEARCH.

Understanding this relationship between solution and price is very important for us as sellers. If we give our buyer a price quote early in the buying cycle when price is of greater concern, the buyer may end the buying cycle without making a purchase. If we wait and give our buyer a quote during SOLUTION SEARCH when price is at its lowest level of concern, we will get fewer price objections. The buyer is able to make a logical decision about price rather than an emotional one.

What causes a buyer to leave SOLUTION SEARCH?

There are two ways buyers leave SOLUTION SEARCH. If the buyer finds a product or service that matches his list of requirements and his budget, he will make his mental decision to buy from that supplier (his *preferred supplier*) and move on to PERCEIVED RISK.

If the buyer decides that he will not find a product to match his list of requirements, he will change to one of two states. If the problem is serious enough, he will change back to NEED EVALUATION and work on redefining his needs. He may be willing to settle for a partial solution, or he may find a completely different way of solving his problem. If the buyer decides that he can live with his problem until a better product is available, he will rationalize his need away and change states to UN-NEED. He will remain there until something or someone else triggers his UN-NEED and changes it into a recognized need.

How will the buyer behave toward sellers?

When a buyer is in SOLUTION SEARCH, he is attempting to match a product to his list of requirements. During this buying state, the buyer needs information from multiple suppliers. He not only is attempting to find the best product or service to meet his needs, he is also verifying that the requirements are reasonable and the budget is realistic.

Preferred supplier versus everyone else

If the **seller is the** *preferred supplier*, and tries to **match his products to the buyer's list of requirements**, the buyer will likely:

- Be enthusiastic and curious about the seller's products.
- Think of ways to use the seller's product that the seller hadn't anticipated.
- Be willing to spend time to evaluate the seller and his company.
- Include the decision maker in appropriate meetings.
- Return the seller's phone calls quickly.

If the seller is **not the** *preferred supplier* and tries **to match his products to the buyer's list of requirements without attempting to extend or change the solution**, the buyer will likely:

- Humor the seller, without any real interest.
- Pressure the seller to hurry things along.
- Tell the seller the product contains a feature that he is unsure of but may be willing to live with.
- Tell the seller that he will make the final decision. There is no need to involve the decision maker.
- Return the seller's phone calls quickly—he still needs the *secondary suppliers*.

Behavioral tendencies and buyer behavior

During SOLUTION SEARCH, we try to match our product to the buyer's requirements. There are many different ways to do this. We choose the best method based on our product or service and the job title of the buyer. A finance executive may want a payback analysis along with a reference's actual return on investment, while a marketing executive might prefer a visit to a reference site. If your product is highly technical, the technical approvers may want several different steps. These could include a product demonstration, a site visit, and a pilot program. Another factor in this buying state is the behavioral style of your buyer. Here's what you can expect from the four behavioral styles during SOLUTION SEARCH.

D's are still interested in results. They may want to talk to a reference account to verify that the reference was able to achieve the desired results. If you do give a product demonstration to a D, you'll want to make sure that it is focused on the issues that are important to your buyer. D's want a product or application overview, not an in-depth understanding of how the product works.

I's will appreciate testimonials from other buyers. If the testimonials are from a well-known person or company, they will value it even more. I's are looking for ways to enhance their position in their own company. They will also be interested in anything that makes their job easier. Try to show them how buying your product can help them achieve their personal and social goals. Keep both of these things in mind when you give I's a product demonstration—show them how easy your product is to use and how much everyone will appreciate them for bringing it into their company.

S's are afraid of change and what it can do to their routine. They will want proof that you can support them after the sale is made. References who can reassure them about the implementation process and help them believe the transition will be smooth are important for S's. If you are trying to extend the solution with an S, give him time to think about the new ideas. If you are giving him a product demonstration, emphasize how quickly users will learn the new system. Emphasize the similarities between the way things are done today and the new way you are proposing. Because of the interest in implementation, you will have an increased opportunity to sell services to S's. Services that help the transition period run smoothly will be beneficial to them.

C's will want the most detailed information of any of the behavioral styles. They emphasize quality and accuracy, and they will want to see evidence of this during SOLUTION SEARCH. C's will be interested in an in-depth demonstration of your product. They may ask detailed questions about your manufacturing process, your support staff, and your current customers. They will be interested in a reference account, but don't expect them to take the reference's word that everything works great. They will want to see it for themselves. When C's ask you questions, you'll want to answer as accurately and with as much detail as possible.

PERCEIVED RISK

PERCEIVED RISK is a difficult area for most sellers, even though it is a natural part of the buying process, because they don't always see it. PERCEIVED RISK is really an emotional struggle that takes place inside the buyer's mind. The buyer has made his mental decision and knows who his *preferred supplier* is. During PER-CEIVED RISK, he has to decide if he should go through with the sale. In order to make this decision, the buyer asks himself, "What could go wrong?" Here's how this state looks to the seller:

> Maria, our seller, has just left Mark's office. She has convinced Mark that her product matches his list of requirements, and the only thing left for Mark to do is to place an order. Maria is very confident that she will receive Mark's purchase order next week.
>
> The following week, Maria doesn't hear from Mark. She decides to call him on Wednesday, but she is told he's in a meeting. She leaves a message, but Mark doesn't return her call that day. On Thursday, she begins to worry. She calls again, and this time she's told that he's on the other line. She leaves another message, and when he doesn't call her back right away, she's convinced he decided to buy from someone else.

What should Maria do? If she's like most sales people, her first instinct is to lower the price, hoping that a lower price will win him back. But think about it—if Mark is in PERCEIVED RISK, he is thinking about all the things that can go wrong. If Maria lowers the price, will that reassure Mark, or will he worry more? Most of the time, lowering the price reinforces the risk feelings, and the seller loses the sale. Of course, this convinces Maria that her instincts were correct. The buyer buys from someone else.

What's really happening here? Why didn't Mark return Maria's calls? Research tells us that buyers only go through PERCEIVED RISK with their *preferred supplier*. That means that the only supplier and product they'll worry about is the one they want. All the other suppliers think the buyer is still in SOLUTION SEARCH because they haven't seen anything change. This period of "non-contact" that Maria experienced is very common. Recall your own house buying experience. Did you want your real estate agent pressuring you while you were trying to decide if you should make an offer on your favorite house? That's exactly how our buyers feel. All buyers go through PERCEIVED RISK alone. Until they've made their decision, they'd rather not talk to their sales person.

What is the buyer thinking about?

At this step in the process, our buyer has decided on a single supplier. Her biggest concern is now her perceived risk. Behavioral scientists tell us there are five types of perceived risk. They are:

1. **Monetary risk**. Here buyers worry that they will lose money if they take action.
2. **Functional risk**. With this type of risk, buyers are concerned that the product won't live up to the claims made by the seller.
3. **Physical risk**. Physical danger is the concern of buyers with this type of risk.

4. **Social risk**. Buyers face this when they are concerned about what their friends and family will think if they make a purchase.

5. **Psychological risk**. This risk deals with feelings of guilt or inadequacy that might occur if a purchase is made.

We can't predict what type of perceived risk our buyer will experience; we know it will be her primary concern. She may worry about the stability of your company, the size of your support staff, or the size of the investment required and the state of the economy. If you sell a technical product, her biggest concern may be that a newer, faster, better product will be released two months after she buys your product. The secondary concern of our buyer is the final cost of your product. Up to this point, our buyer has dealt with the price of your product. She used this as a guideline for payback analysis and investment required. Now she is concerned with the final cost—what she will actually pay for your product or service. This is where our buyer will initiate price negotiation. Our buyer's third concern is details of the solution, a low priority because of the time she spent dealing with her need in SOLUTION SEARCH. Our buyer's lowest concern is her need because she dealt with it during NEED EVALUATION and SOLUTION SEARCH.

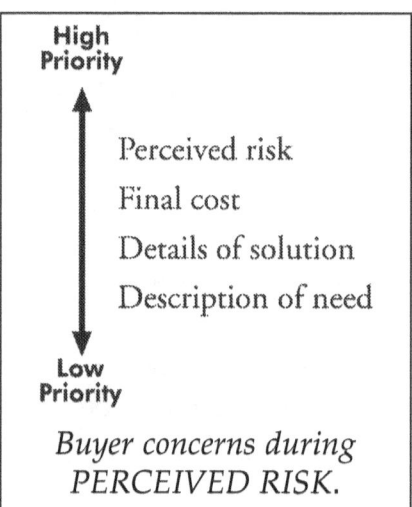

High Priority

Perceived risk

Final cost

Details of solution

Description of need

Low Priority

Buyer concerns during PERCEIVED RISK.

What causes a buyer to leave PERCEIVED RISK?

There are several ways buyers will leave PERCEIVED RISK. If they decide that the risk is too great, their action will depend on what type of risk they find. If the risk concerns their *preferred supplier,* they may decide not to purchase from that supplier. If this happens, they may change back to SOLUTION SEARCH and take another look at their *secondary suppliers*. If the risk is based on the product itself, they may change back to NEED EVALUATION and redefine their needs. If the risk is based on the purchase, they may decide that the timing isn't right, and they will change back to UN-NEED until something else reminds them of their problem or the circumstances change.

When buyers go through PERCEIVED RISK and decide that the value of the product is worth the risk, they will make the purchase. At this point, our buyer will change states to NO NEED. She will stay in NO NEED until something changes to create a new need.

How will the buyer behave toward sellers?

Buyers in PERCEIVED RISK are trying to anticipate everything that might go wrong. How buyers express their concerns will vary depending on their behavioral tendencies. However, there are some commonalities in how buyers react to their *preferred supplier* and *secondary suppliers* during PERCEIVED RISK.

Preferred supplier versus everyone else

If the **seller is the** *preferred supplier* and the **buyer has made his mental decision to buy from the seller**, the buyer will likely:
- Focus on risk objections rather than product objections.
- Be willing to schedule the seller first and last for final presentations.
- Go through a period of "non-contact" where he won't want to see or talk to the seller.
- Include the decision maker in appropriate meetings.

If the **seller is not the** *preferred supplier* and **the buyer has made his mental decision to buy from someone else**, the buyer will likely:
- Give the seller lots of encouragement until the end.

- Return the seller's phone calls quickly because the buyer still needs the *secondary suppliers*.
- Try to get the seller to lower the price without telling who has the order.
- Keep the seller away from the decision maker.
- When it's over, tell the seller he lost because of a feature, not because someone else sold better than he did.

Behavioral tendencies and buyer behavior

The only time we will see our buyer going through PERCEIVED RISK is when we are the *preferred supplier*. The four behavioral styles will express their risk concerns differently. How you as the seller answer will depend on your buyer's profile. Be very careful if the concerns relate to the state of the economy, business or government politics or technology improvements. If you try to answer these concerns, your buyer won't believe you because you don't have the experience or expertise. (Our best economists can't tell us what's going to happen, why should you?)

D's will be very direct when they tell you their concern. Don't be offended, that's their natural way of communicating. They want reassurance from you that they will be able to achieve the results that they want. Show them how you can help them with this. D's put feelings and opinions at a low priority, so now is not the time to express yours. They like change and challenge, so help them see how the risk they fear is really a challenge.

I's are uncomfortable with conflict and, as a result, do not respond well to an aggressive close. They will share their feelings with you concerning risk. They want empathy from you, as well as reassurance that others in the same situation have been successful. I's are concerned with how others view them. Remind them that they will be viewed as the person who solved an expensive problem for their company. I's love innovation and change, so help them see how their decision brings about both for their company.

S's may not tell you their real concern. You may have to ask questions to uncover what is really bothering them. S's try to avoid risk at all cost. Since they are concerned with the implementation and support, now is the time to reassure them by reviewing the steps involved in making the transition and the support options your company offers. S's do not like to be rushed in their decision-making. Make sure you give them enough time to think it over.

C's like to kill change with logic and information. They will need the most proof during SOLUTION SEARCH. The more attention you pay to their concerns during SOLUTION SEARCH, the less trouble you will have during PERCEIVED RISK. When C's feel like their questions weren't answered or their requests were ignored, they will do everything in their power to kill the sale. Answer their questions with logic and facts. Give them evidence to counteract their risk concerns.

Self Test

The following case studies describe a single individual. Read the case study, identify the buying state, and decide what your next step would be. Then answer the questions below each case study.

Michael Rodriguez

Michael Rodriguez calls you to tell you that he is getting ready to buy a product similar to yours. He would like you to come out and tell him about your product as well as give him a price quote because he is in a hurry to buy.

1. What buying state is Michael in?
   a. NO NEED.
   b. UN-NEED.
   c. NEED EVALUATION.
   d. SOLUTION SEARCH.
   e. PERCEIVED RISK.

2. How would you respond? Do you:
   a. Make an appointment for the next day and prepare a price quotation, as he requested.
   b. Find out what features he needs, so you can verify that your product will work for him.
   c. Find out how he intends to use the product, so you know what capabilities he needs.
   d. Tell him about capabilities your product has that your competitors don't have.
   e. Find out how he intends to use the product, so you know what capabilities he needs, then try to extend the solution with additional capabilities.

Sara Chan

You have been working with Sara Chan for 3 months. Last week she told you that she would make her decision this week. Up to this point, you've had a very friendly relationship with her, and you were convinced she was going to buy from you after your last meeting. But this week, you suspect something has changed. She hasn't returned your call from yesterday morning.

3. What buying state is Sara in?
   a. NO NEED.
   b. UN-NEED.
   c. NEED EVALUATION.
   d. SOLUTION SEARCH.
   e. PERCEIVED RISK.

4. How would you respond? Do you:
   a. Call every ten minutes, ready to offer her a larger discount if she'll buy from you.
   b. Relax and let her call you. You're confident you're still the *preferred supplier*.
   c. Go call on her in person. She won't refuse to see you if you're at her office.
   d. Have your boss call. Maybe bringing in the "big guns" will help.
   e. Give up. You've lost the sale anyway.

6.   Getting started

Why is this information important?

Every buyer with every purchase experiences the buying process described. With small purchases or inexpensive products, it may be difficult to recognize each buying state. With larger purchases or expensive products, it is easier to recognize the individual buying states.

We encourage you to analyze your own purchases and determine your thoughts and experiences as you move through the buying process. Once you understand your own buying process and you recognize when you are in a specific state, you will find it easier to recognize those same states in other people.

Understanding where a buyer is in the buying process can help you determine the appropriate actions that will make the buyer most comfortable. You will be able to determine what buyers need from you at each step, based on their behavioral tendencies and buying state.

Where to go from here

These next sections are intended to help you internalize the information you've just read. Since this information is intended for a variety of people, each with a different job in your organization, we have divided the material according to job function. Please read the material and follow the instructions to develop your own personal action plan for each applicable section.

Everyone in an organization

You have an opportunity to use the information on how buyers buy, no matter what position you currently hold in your organization. Since the easiest way to learn the buying states is to analyze your personal buying experiences, that is the first step in committing this information to memory. As you work with potential customers, try to determine their buying state, as well as their behavioral style. If you remember your concerns and priorities as you moved through the buying states, you'll have a better understanding of what's important to your buyer.

For each group of questions, you will be asked to think of situations where you are a buyer. It doesn't matter whether the purchase is something you are presently contemplating or something that has already occurred. Both situations will help you learn the buying states.

You as a late market buyer

Think of a buying situation where you were buying a product that "everyone else" already had. Now answer the questions below.
1. What was the product?
2. Why did you not buy this product earlier?
3. What motivated you to finally buy the product?
4. List your considerations during NEED EVALUATION (when you were trying to decide if you really needed to buy it).
5. How many products did you look at during SOLUTION SEARCH?
6. Did your requirements change after looking at several products?
7. Describe any behaviors exhibited by a sales person that you disliked.

8. What specific types of PERCEIVED RISK did you consider before making your purchasing decision?

You as an inexpert buyer

Think of a buying situation where you were buying a product that you didn't understand. Now answer the questions below.
1. What was the product?
2. Whose information about the product did you find most helpful?
3. Did you believe everything the sales people told you? Explain.
4. List your considerations during NEED EVALUATION (when you were trying to decide if you really needed to buy it).
5. How many products did you look at during SOLUTION SEARCH?
6. Did your requirements change after looking at several products? How?
7. Describe any undesirable behaviors exhibited by a sales person.
8 What specific types of PERCEIVED RISK did you consider before making your purchasing decision?

You as an early market buyer

Think of a buying situation where you were one of the first people to buy a product. Now answer the questions below.
1. What was the product?
2. What first caught your attention?
3. What motivated you to buy the product?
4. List your considerations during NEED EVALUATION (when you were trying to decide if you really needed to buy it).
5. How many products did you look at during SOLUTION SEARCH?
6. Did your requirements change after evaluating other products?
7. Describe any behaviors exhibited by a sales person that you disliked.
8. What specific types of PERCEIVED RISK did you consider before making your purchasing decision?

You as an expert buyer

Think of a buying situation where you were buying a product that you understand thoroughly. Now answer the questions below.

1. What was the product?
2. Did you need anyone's help in determining why you should make the purchase?
3. Did you want to spend time explaining to the sales person why you need the product?
4. List your considerations during NEED EVALUATION (when you were trying to decide if you really needed to buy it).
5. How many products did you look at during SOLUTION SEARCH?
6. Did your requirements change after looking at several products? How?
7. Describe any behaviors exhibited by a sales person that you disliked.
8. What specific types of PERCEIVED RISK did you consider before making your purchasing decision?

The next step

How you use this information will vary depending on your job function within your organization. We've provided several examples of how others have used this information. You may think of additional ways it can help you.

If you produce marketing materials

If you produce any type of marketing material, the best way to start using this material is to analyze your current marketing collateral. There are several things to look for when you produce advertising, brochures, direct mail pieces or trade show strategies. Ask yourself these questions:

- Who is your target market?
- Is your prospect an early market or late market buyer?
- What level in an organization are you targeting? Will you reach *shoppers* or *decision-makers*?
- What buying state will your prospect be in when he or she receives this material?
- Does it help buyers in UN-NEED recognize or acknowledge their need?

Existing advertisement

Select a current advertisement, and answer the following questions.
1. Briefly describe the advertisement you have chosen.
2. Is it designed for early market or late market buyers?
3. Does it appeal to expert or inexpert buyers?
4. What level in your prospect's organization would most likely be interested?
5. In which buying state will your prospect likely be if he or she answers this advertisement?
6. What changes would you make to improve this advertisement?

Existing brochure

Select a current brochure, and answer the following questions.
1. Briefly describe the brochure you have chosen.
2. Is it designed for early market or late market buyers?
3. Does it appeal to expert or inexpert buyers?
4. What level in your prospect's organization would most likely be interested?
5. In which buying state will your prospect be when he or she receives this material?
6. What changes would you make to improve this material?

Existing direct mail piece

Select a current direct mail piece, and answer the following questions.
1. Briefly describe the direct mail piece you have chosen.
2. Is it designed for early market or late market buyers?
3. Does it appeal to expert or inexpert buyers?
4. What level in your prospect's organization would most likely be interested?
5. What buying state will your prospect be in when he or she receives this material?
6. What changes would you make to improve this material?

Existing trade show strategy

Evaluate your existing trade show strategy by answering the following questions.
1. Briefly describe the trade show strategy you have chosen.
2. Is it designed for early market or late market buyers?
3. Does it appeal to expert or inexpert buyers?
4. What level in your prospect's organization would most likely be interested?
5. In which buying state will your prospect be when he or she sees your booth?
6. What changes would you make to reach your target market?

Future materials

Now that you've had a chance to analyze your current marketing materials, we'd like you to spend a few minutes thinking about what a sales person needs throughout the buying process. What is the buying state of the prospect, what are the prospective buyer's biggest concerns, and what does the sales person need to answer those concerns?

Visualize your ideal marketing program, designed to help the sales person and buyer throughout the entire buying process. Now answer the following questions.

1. Buyer's in UN-NEED have very little interest in your product. What type of information would be interesting?
2. How can you use your answer from question number 1 in:
   - a direct mail piece?
   - an advertisement?
   - a trade show booth?
   - a brochure?
3. What type of information do buyers in NEED EVALUATION want from your company?
4. What type of information do buyers in SOLUTION SEARCH want from your company?

If you are in customer service

If you are in customer service, you can use this information in two ways. First, if you can recognize the behavioral style of your customer, you can improve your communication and have a higher customer satisfaction rating.

Second, you can help your sales organization recognize need very early in the buying process. Since you are in customer service, you are in a position to recognize buyers in UN-NEED and NEED EVALUATION when they call in for help, long before they ever call a sales person. Because buyers buy to satisfy needs, the earlier you can recognize these needs, the greater your success will be.

To help you with behavior style identification and need recognition, answer the following questions.

Customer #1

Bob telephones you with a problem. He talks fast, and he doesn't appear to have any interest in socializing. He's all business. After you help him solve his initial problem, he begins to tell you about another difficulty he's currently experiencing. You realize that another product your company sells would help with this new issue.

1. Bob's most likely behavioral style is:
   a. D
   b. I
   c. S
   d. C

2. What is the best way to help Bob with a problem or request?
   a. Spend a lot of time giving him a detailed answer to his question.
   b. Answer his questions quickly and concisely.
   c. Be willing to spend some time on small talk. Show him you empathize with his problem as you help him solve it.
   d. All of the above.

3. Once you realize that your company sells a product that might help Bob, do you:
   a. Tell Bob what you know about the product.
   b. Offer to send him literature about the product.
   c. Write down his problem, name, company name, and contact information, and then call the appropriate sales person with this information.
   d. Ignore the problem. After all, you did what you were supposed to do; you helped him with the reason he called.
   e. None of the above.

Customer #2

Teresa calls you with a problem. She is very friendly, and interjects small talk in between her description of her problem. She's very enthusiastic and begins to tell you about another department at her company that could use your product.

1. Teresa's most likely behavioral style is:
   a. D
   b. I
   c. S
   d. C

2. What is the best way to help Teresa with a problem or request?
   a. Spend a lot of time giving her a detailed answer to her question.
   b. Answer her questions quickly and concisely.
   c. Be willing to spend some time on small talk. Show her you empathize with her problem as you help her solve it.
   d. All of the above.

3. How do you handle the referral from Teresa, do you:
   a. Tell Teresa all about the product so she can tell her other department.
   b. Offer to send her literature about the product so Teresa can pass it along.
   c. Write down the name, company name, department name and contact information, along with Teresa's name as the person who gave the referral, then call the appropriate sales person with this information.
   d. Ignore it. It's not your job to find new business. That's what the sales people are paid to do.
   e. None of the above.

Determining your customer's behavioral style

Choose three customers, either internal or external, with whom you have frequent contact and answer the questions below.
1. Name of the first person:
   a. What is his or her most likely behavioral style?
   b. How can you modify your communication style to make him or her more comfortable?

2. Name of the second person:
   a. What is his or her most likely behavioral style?
   b. How can you modify your communication style to make him or her more comfortable?

3. Name of the third person:
   a. What is his or her most likely behavioral style?
   b. How can you modify your communication style to make him or her more comfortable?

If you are in sales

If you are in sales, you will have many opportunities to use this information. Understanding your prospect's buying state will help you determine your most effective action. You will learn to recognize when you are the *preferred supplier* and when you are one of several *secondary suppliers*. As you become more comfortable with the buying states, you'll learn how to recognize risk and the non-contact period that often occurs.

As you meet new people, you will be able to determine their behavioral style. This information will help you modify your communication methods. You'll find that you learn more information from people when you treat them the way they prefer to be treated.

In order to help you apply this information, please answer the questions that follow.

Prospect in the beginning of the buying process

Pick a prospect with whom you have just started working and answer the following questions.

1. Name of prospect:
2. What is this person's most likely behavioral style?
3. What is this person's current buying state?
4. What information does this buyer need from you during this state?
5. Are you the *preferred supplier* or a *secondary supplier*? How can you tell?
6. Is your prospect an early market buyer or a late market buyer? Why?
7. Is your prospect an expert buyer, or an inexpert buyer? Why?
8. What can you do to adapt your behavior to this person?

Prospect in the middle of the buying process

Choose a prospect that is in the middle of the buying and answer the following questions.

1. Name of prospect:
2. What is this person's most likely behavioral style?
3. What is this person's current buying state?
4. What information does this buyer need from you during this state?
5. Are you the *preferred supplier* or a *secondary supplier*? How can you tell?
6. Is your prospect an early market buyer or a late market buyer? Why?
7. Is your prospect an expert buyer, or an inexpert buyer? Why?
8. What can you do to adapt your behavior to this person?

Prospect toward the end of the buying process

Choose a prospect near the end of the buying process and answer the following questions.

1. Name of prospect:
2. What is this person's most likely behavioral style?
3. What is this person's current buying state?

4. What information does this buyer need from you during this state?
5. Are you the *preferred supplier* or a *secondary supplier*? How can you tell?
6. Is your prospect an early market buyer or a late market buyer? Why?
7. Is your prospect an expert buyer, or an inexpert buyer? Why?
8. What can you do to adapt your behavior to this person?

Answers to Self Tests

Chapter 1

1. If we understand how buyers buy, we will be able to match our actions with the buyer's needs. This information can help us whether we are in sales, marketing, customer support, or any other group that deals directly with customers.

2. Because there are unethical sales people who try to force buyers to buy their products, buyers are skeptical when they meet any new sales person. Most buyers have bought something because a sales person convinced them that it would solve a problem, only to find that the product didn't work the way it was promised. The stereotype of the used car sales person is so well known and present everywhere, that most people expect the stereotype rather than being surprised by it.

Chapter 2

1. Answer will be based on your personal experiences.

2. Companies work with multiple suppliers in order to: verify that the product is the best fit for the application, verify that the product is reasonably priced, ensure that they have a fall-

back plan if the primary supplier drops out, and negotiate the best price.

3. **Shopper**: a person who is interested in your company or your products but has not admitted a business problem to you.
   Prospect: a person who has admitted a business problem to you, but has not yet agreed to arrange a meeting with the next level up in the approval process.
   Promoter: a person who has admitted a business problem to you and has agreed to arrange a meeting with the next level up in the decision making process.
   Decision-maker: a person who has either the authority or the influence to cause an unbudgeted purchase of your products or services. They must have admitted a business problem to you. They should be able to arrange a meeting with anyone in the company with whom you would like to speak.

Chapter 3

1. Answer will be based on your personal experiences.

2. Answer will be based on your personal experiences.

3. Yes, because when the buyer understands the product, he doesn't need the seller to help supply the logical reasons for the purchase. He knows he can buy the same product from several different suppliers, so the relationship between the buyer and the seller becomes part of the purchasing decision. The buyer looks to the seller for the emotional reasons to buy.

Chapter 4

1. What the product or service will do for them.

2. Who else is using the product or service, and what they say about it.

3. How the product or service will help stabilize conditions for them.

4. Why the product or service is a logical investment for them.

5. D's are change-agents because they are most interested in results. Something must change in order to achieve results, so they like to instigate change.
6. I's are change-creators because they like to be all things to all people. They don't like routine, so they will stir things up when they get bored. They are easily distracted, so they don't always follow through on the change they create.

7. S's are change-resistors because they value stability. They like things to stay the same and as a result do not like change.

8. C's are change-terminators because they value accuracy and order. They want to be positive before taking any action that causes change. Since this is nearly impossible, C's will kill change whenever they can.

Chapter 5

1. d.
2. e.
3. e.
4. b.

Chapter 6

All answers from this module will come from your own personal experiences.

Topical Index

Selected Bibliography

Adams, J., J. Hayes, and B. Hopson. *Transitions—Understanding and Managing Personal Change*. Oxford, England: Martin Robertson, 1976.

Alessandra, Tony, and Michael J. O'Conner. *The Platinum Rule*. New York: Warner Books, 1996.

Bosworth, Michael T. *Solution Selling*. Burr Ridge, Illinois: Irwin Professional Publishing, 1995.

Cartwright, Roger, Michael Collins, George Green, and Anita Candy. *In Charge of Yourself*. Cambridge, Massachusettes: Blackwell Business Publishers, 1996.

Davis, Kevin. *Getting Into Your Customer's Head*. New York: Times Books, 1996.

Moore, Geoffrey A. *Crossing the Chasm*. Harper Business, 1991.

Rackham, Neil. *SPIN Selling*. New York: McGraw-Hill Book Company, 1988.

Robbins, Stephen P. *Organizational Behavior*. Englewood Cliffs, New Jersey: Prentice Hall, 1996.

Robbins, Harvey and Michael Finley. *Why Change Doesn't Work*. Princeton, New Jersey: Peterson's, 1996.

Trout, Jack, with Steve Rivkin. *The New Positioning*. New York: McGraw-Hill Book Company, 1996.

0-595-29462-6